Branches
of the
Military

Sean
Callery

SCHOLASTIC INC.
New York   Toronto   London   Auckland
Sydney   Mexico City   New Delhi   Hong Kong

Read more! Do more!

After you read this book, download your free all-new digital activities.

You can show what a great reader you are!

For Mac and PC

Take quizzes about the facts in this book.

Do fun activities with simple step-by-step instructions!

Log on to

www.scholastic.com/discovermore/readers

Enter this special code: **L2BMMRC9XFK2**

Contents

EDUCATIONAL BOARD:
Monique Datta, EdD, Asst. Professor, Rossier School of Education, USC;
Karyn Saxon, PhD, Elementary Curriculum Coordinator, Wayland, MA;
Francie Alexander, Chief Academic Officer, Scholastic Inc.

ISBN 978-0-545-68101-8

12 11 10 9 8 7 6 5 4 3 2 1   15 16 17 18 19 20/0

Printed in the U.S.A.   40
This edition first printing, January 2015

Scholastic is constantly working to lessen the environmental
impact of our manufacturing processes. To view our
industry-leading paper procurement policy,
visit www.scholastic.com/paperpolicy.

The US military

Sometimes we must stand up for what is right. The US military is one of the biggest, strongest fighting forces in the world.

Army
Army soldiers are ready to fight at all times. They are strong in body and mind.

Marine Corps
The Marines are the first to fight in times of danger. They can handle anything.

It's a fact!

Who is the person in charge of the

Navy

The Navy fights on and under the oceans. Its sailors patrol the waters around the world.

Air Force

The job of the Air Force is to fly, fight, and win. Its planes can attack anywhere.

Coast Guard

The Coast Guard protects our waters. Its rescue teams save people in danger in the water.

Army

Every soldier in the Army has an important job. The officers are the leaders. Officers and soldiers work together to get jobs done. They are loyal to one another and to their country.

NEW WORD

loyal
LOI-uhl
The Army's **loyal** soldiers obey orders.

SAY IT OUT LOUD

Army soldiers may travel in Air Force planes.

A tank is a tough vehicle. It protects soldiers.

7

New soldiers are called recruits. They go to boot camp for ten weeks of training. A drill sergeant tells them how to follow orders and prepare for battle.

NEW WORD

recruit
ri-KROOT
A **recruit** is a new member of the armed forces.

SAY IT OUT LOUD

Recruits are tested on push-ups,

Soon after arriving, male recruits get their hair cut short.

Training tests their speed and strength.

Recruits have to do lots of tough exercises.

Huff! Puff! Recruits learn how to work together as a team.

sit-ups, and how fast they can run.

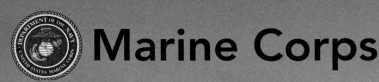

Marine Corps

No one knows where the next battle may be. The military needs a force that can respond quickly and take control when it gets there. That's the Marines.

Recruits do basic training for 12 weeks, then train some more to be ready to defend their nation and one another.

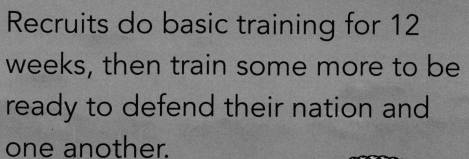

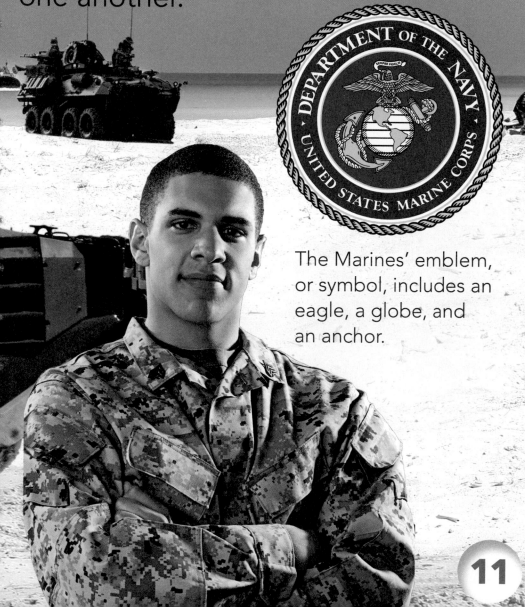

The Marines' emblem, or symbol, includes an eagle, a globe, and an anchor.

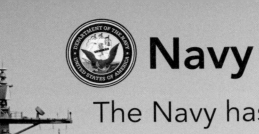

Navy

The Navy has 293 ships. Aircraft carriers carry Navy planes. They are like floating airports.

There are many kinds of Navy ships.

Littoral combat ship

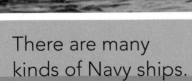

Frigate

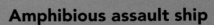

Amphibious assault ship

Destroyers and cruisers are fast ships. Submarines hide by moving below the waves.

Aircraft carrier

Cruiser

Destroyer

Submarine

Once, only men could serve in the military. Now women can serve, too. Women train as hard as men do. They are in on the action. Women can be Navy pilots, doctors, or engineers.

On the Same Team

Enlist in the **WAVES**

APPLY TO YOUR NEAREST
NAVY RECRUITING STATION OR OFFICE OF NAVAL OFFICER PROCUREMENT

Women first served in the Navy in the same way as men during World Wars I and II.

It's a fact!

Of the 1.4 million people in the US

Admiral Michelle Howard is the Navy's first female four-star admiral.

Air Force

The Air Force has more than 5,600 planes. Fighter planes are very fast. Pilots can twist and turn them in the air. Spy planes check out what the enemy is doing.

F-22 Raptor
fighter plane

B-2 Spirit
stealth bomber

U-2 spy plane

The F-22 Raptor can fly over 1,400 miles per hour.

The Air Force is high-tech! It has planes that don't even need pilots! The Air Force also sends satellites into space. These can spot enemy action. Forces on the ground use them to find their way around, too. This is called using GPS.

GPS
receiver

It's a
fact!

The military relies on technology.

Rockets launch
satellites into space.

Satellites travel
around Earth.

It was using computers almost 70 years ago!

Coast Guard

The men and women of the Coast Guard are always ready. They are always ready to protect ports, rivers, and coasts.

They find and save people who are in trouble in the water.

In the air
The Coast Guard has more than 200 planes.

NEW WORD
port
port
Boats and ships can dock safely in **ports**.
SAY IT OUT LOUD

On the water
Coast Guard boats are between 12 and 65 feet long.

21

To the rescue! A boat is sinking. The Coast Guard's HH-65 Dolphin helicopter gets moving. Every second counts! Two people are floating in the water. They are wearing life jackets. A rescue swimmer comes down a cable. He helps the people into a rescue basket. They are pulled up to safety. Job done!

It's a fact!

On average, the Coast Guard

saves ten lives every day.

Military uniforms

It is an honor to wear a military uniform. Each branch has a combat uniform for battle. A Marine's combat uniform provides good camouflage. It's hard to see a Marine on the battlefield.

A vest protects a Marine from bullets.

Can you spot the Marines?

The helmet is large and light.

The shirt has four pockets.

The tan boots grip surfaces.

A dress uniform is worn for special occasions. Medals and ribbons may be awards for brave actions in battle.

Marines

Army

Coast Guard

Air Force

Navy

Why we serve

The members of every branch of the military think they have the best jobs. They are serving their country. And they get to see the rest of the world!

Major Cedric L. Burden served in the US Army in Iraq. He says: "It's important to support soldiers, sailors, Marines, and airmen. Freedom isn't free, and someone has to do hard things during hard times."

Glossary

admiral
A top officer in the Navy or Coast Guard.

aircraft carrier
A ship with a large, flat deck where planes and helicopters take off and land.

boot camp
A program in which new recruits learn how to serve in the military.

cable
A strong metal rope.

camouflage
A pattern or disguise that helps people and objects blend in with what is around them.

defend
To protect.

drill sergeant
A person in the Army who trains new recruits.

emblem
A symbol or sign that stands for something.

force
A group of people who work together, especially in the military.

GPS
A system of satellites and tools that tells people where they are and how to get somewhere. *GPS* stands for *Global Positioning System.*

helicopter
A flying vehicle with large spinning blades on top.

life jacket
A vest that keeps a person afloat in the water.

loyal
Always faithful and supportive.

major
A type of officer in the Army, Marine Corps, or Air Force.

officer
A person in the military who is in charge.

patrol
To watch and protect an area.

pilot
A person who flies a plane.

port
A place where boats and ships can stay safely.

recruit
A new member of the military.

rescue basket
A basket lowered from a helicopter to rescue a person. The person gets in the basket and is lifted into the helicopter.

rocket
A vehicle with a very powerful engine that travels into space.

satellite
A spacecraft that travels around Earth and sends information back.

serve
To do work that helps others; for example, to be in the military.

spy plane
A plane with cameras and other tools that can secretly gather information.

submarine
A ship that travels underwater.

Index

Images

Defense Imagery: 6 bg, 7 bg (Spc Tristan Bolden), cover cl, cover r, 21 b inset, 28 b inset; Dreamstime: 26 stars, 27 stars (Alesaggio), 17 tl silhouette (Maxfx), 4 bg, 5 bg (Mcpics), cover c face (Mimagephotography), cover t bg (Robodread), 16 t silhouette (Steve Mann), 26 bg, 27 bg (Vacclav); DVIDS: back cover t (Petty Officer 1st Class Adam Eggers), cover cr (Petty Officer Nick Ameen), 17 tr silhouette; Getty Images/Stocktrek Images: 16 main, 17 main; iStockphoto: inside front cover b (artbyjulie), cover l, 11 b fg (DanielBendjy), inside front cover t (filo), silhouette soldier throughout, 22 br silhouette (Jeremy), 22 bg, 23 bg (malerapaso), cartoon soldier throughout (mocoo), 2 arrows (pagadesign), mud splats throughout (shiny7777), 24 bg (sixdesignstudio), back cover computer, 2 computers (skodonnell), tape throughout (spxChrome); Library of Congress/John Philip Falter: 14 l; Shutterstock, Inc./resnak: 23 b silhouette; Tim Loughhead/Precision Illustration: 12 b silhouettes, 13 b silhouettes; US Navy: 4 cr (Journalist 2nd Class John J. Pistone), 13 t fg (Mass Communication Specialist 2nd Class Dominique Pineiro), 30, 31 (Mass Communication Specialist 3rd Class Scott Fenaroli), 27 b inset (Mass Communication Specialist Seaman Abby Rader), 14 r, 15 bg, 32 (Mass Communication Specialist 2nd Class Carlos M. Vazquez II), 5 tl (Mass Communication Specialist Second Class Stuart Phillips), 4 br (Photographer's Mate Airman Apprentice Shannon Garcia), 12 t bg, 13 t bg (PO1 Shawn Torgerson), cover c uniform, 2 cr, 15 t inset; US Air Force: 7 tl inset (Airman 1st Class Trevor Rhynes), 19 bg (Bill Hartenstein/United Launch Alliance), 27 c inset (SSgt Sheila de Vera), 18 fg (Staff Sgt David Carbajal), 18 bg (Sue Sapp), 5 cl, 19 t inset; US Army: 7 b fg (Sgt Michael Uribe), 7 tr inset, 8, 9 c, 9 tr, 27 tl inset, 28 bg, 29; US Coast Guard: 22 c inset (PA1 Kurt Fredrickson), 20 fg (Petty Officer 1st Class Brandyn Hill), 22 l inset (Petty Officer 2nd Class LaNola Stone), 20 bg, 21 bg (Petty Officer 3rd Class Anthony L. Soto), 21 t inset (Photographer's Mate 1st Class Keith W. DeVinney), 27 tr inset (Senior Chief Petty Officer), 22 r inset (Tsgt Edward Gyokeres), 2 cl, 5 bl, 9 tl, 23 fg; US Department of Defense: military emblems throughout; US Marines: 25 c inset (Cpl Antwuan Jefferson), 10 bg beach, 11 bg beach (Cpl Theodore W. Ritchie), 1 (Lance Cpl Cory D. Polom), 24 r inset (Sgt Ethan Rocke), 25 b inset (Sgt Justis Beauregard), 26 fg (Sgt Randall Clinton), 11 tl fg, 25 bg (Sgt Austin Hazard), 25 t inset (Sgt Christopher O'Quin), 3, 9 tc, 10 fg, 24 l inset.

Thank you

For his generosity of time in sharing his expertise, special thanks to Petty Officer First Class Patrick A. Long, USN (Retired).